UNUSUAL HOTELS

WORLD

JONGLEZ PUBLISHING

CONTENTS

AMERICA

EUROPE

© Mallory Owen

Free Spirit Spheres

Living in and among the trees

Eve, Eryn and Melody are three spherical tree houses suspended in a patch of Vancouver Island forest. Even the smallest (single-person-sized), Eve, provides guests with a spiritual connection to the forest. These spheres sway in time with the trees and guests comment on how they encourage creative thought. Eryn is the largest wooden sphere (Melody is fibreglass-built) and sleeps two comfortably, with a third person in a loft bed.

The motion in a sphere is a slow, gentle rocking when the wind blows. The rope tethers are almost vertical, which lets the treetops move considerably while hardly moving the sphere at all.

Beautifully crafted, the joinery is yacht-style with brass trim, varnished wood and cane doors. The tree houses have closets on either side of the door. These function as partial bulkheads to reinforce the door opening as well as adding cupboard space. A shared composting toilet outhouse is located at the base of the spheres.

More traditional facilities are found 60 m (66 yds) from the spheres and include: two washrooms, two showers, a sauna and a covered deck with barbecue and picnicking resources. Bedding and towels are supplied.

Each sphere is wired for power and has built-in speakers for those who wish to bring their own music ... the perfect opportunity to experience true surround sound.

Longer rentals are offered as well as the opportunity to purchase a pre-built sphere of your own.

Quinta Real Zacatecas

Bullring converted to luxury hotel

Beef is back on the menu at the Plaza de Toros San Pedro. While it no longer showcases the matador's skills, this bullring, built in 1866, faced demolition when it closed in 1975. Thankfully state laws recognized it as a historic monument, but it remained idle in a state of decay until Quinta Real started a two-year reconstruction, finally opening the hotel to guests in 1989. Accolades and plaudits from architects, travellers and those seeking an extraordinary venue have followed the sympathetic reconstruction.

The city itself is a colonial attraction, with many historic and cultural sights, however, it is the bullring that dominates downtown.

Quinta Real Zacatecas is both a top-class hotel and historic monument in one. The rooms look inwards to the plaza and, although luxurious, are conservatively but comfortably furnished and cannot be considered unusual. The bar, however, starts to highlight the building's heritage, as it is located in the original bull pens. The tiered restaurant – a nightmare for waiters having to weave in and out of secluded alcove tables and up and down many staircases, is built into the original walls, where once crowds used to watch the spectacle. Now guests are more likely to preside over weddings and cultural events, using the bullring itself for dinners and galas.

Costa Verde

A 727 jet converted into luxury accommodation

Salvaged from its San Jose airport resting place, a refurbished 1965 vintage Boeing 727 airframe has been transported to create a fantastic two-bedroom suite: a favourite for weddings, honeymoons and romance.

Perched on a 15 m (50 ft) pedestal, this classic aircraft offers scenic ocean and jungle views from the hard-wood deck built atop the plane's right wing.

In its former life, the plane flew under the colours of South Africa Air and latterly Avianca Airlines (Colombia).

© David Tipling/Canopy Tower

© RAdP

© David Tipling/Canopy Tower

Canopy Tower

Radar tower hotel provides view of rainforest birds in tree canopy

Built in 1965 by the United States Air Force to house radar used in the defence of the Panama Canal, the tower was demilitarized and transferred to Panama in 1996. Located on top of Semaphore Hill, in the heart of the semi-deciduous Soberanía National Park, it rises above the tree canopy. Dominating the roof is the 9-m-high (30 ft) geotangent dome with an observation deck surrounding it, from which you can see the Pacific entrance to the Panama Canal and the skyline of Panama City. The top floor is used as the main dining area, and is completely surrounded by panoramic windows. The second and first floors provide the living space, with en suite bathrooms and large windows to observe lower levels of the forest canopy.

You are never more than a short distance from the birds and should pack earplugs if you're a light sleeper and don't want to be woken at first light. They wake at dawn on this migratory route and you'll have ample opportunity to see those normally only glimpsed high in the tops of trees, right outside your Canopy Tower room.

Your host is the friendly Raúl Arias de Para, who not only is knowledgeable about the birds and wildlife but tells some great lighthearted stories over evening drinks.

Skylodge Adventure Suites

Transparent capsules hanging from a cliff

In the heart of the Sacred Valley of Cuzco, Peru, the rooms at Skylodge Adventures are spectacular. Clinging to the cliff at an altitude of 400 metres, four futuristic living quarters (whose design is inspired by the aerospace industry) give the unique sensation of experiencing what mountaineers go through during extreme climbs, when they have to suspend their tents above the void, hung with pitons on peaked walls.

Opened in June 2013, the hotel is safely accessible thanks to a team of professional bilingual guides, along a via ferrata or a hike with zip lines.

Three transparent capsules (to better appreciate the view on the valley below) for up to eight people offer overnight stays, but it is also possible to have lunch in the collective capsule. The capsules are solar-powered and the bathrooms have dry toilets. Each capsule can accommodate from one to four people.

Magic Mountain Hotel

Forest accommodation in a fairytale mountain

The Huilo Huilo Biological Reserve has pioneered sustainable tourism in Chile, preserving nature with local community involvement and providing amazing accommodation. Award-winning Montaña Mágica Lodge, Nothofagus Hotel & Spa and Reino Fungi Lodge all have comfortable rooms in surrealist ethnic architectural creations that defy easy classification.

Montaña Mágica Lodge is styled after a fairytale about a magical mountain that grants wishes. With a waterfall cascading from the roof and outside its 13 rooms and suites, the lodge is indeed a special place.

Nothofagus Hotel & Spa is inspired by the Southern Beech and, like a 7-storey tree, has 55 rooms arranged around a central trunk. At 35 m (15 ft) high, the uppermost suites overlook the tree canopy and the Mocho-Chochuenco volcano.

The three floors of Reino Fungi Lodge take the form of a giant mushroom offering 11 rooms. Its glass-covered central core provides natural lighting and showcases an oak tree that is already taller than the lodge itself.

5 PENZANC

The Egyptian House

Celebration of Napoleonic success in Egypt

Of a style in vogue after Napoleon's 1798 Egypt campaign, the Egyptian House dates from about 1835. The front elevation is very similar to that of the former Egyptian Hall in Piccadilly, designed in 1812 by P. F. Robinson. Robinson or Foulston of Plymouth are the most likely candidates for its design, although there is no evidence to support the claim of either. It was built for John Lavin as a museum and geological repository. Bought by The Landmark Trust in 1968, its colossal façade, with lotus-bud capitals and enrichments of Coade stone, concealed two small granite houses above shops, solid and with a pleasant rear elevation, but very decrepit inside. These were reconstructed into three compact apartments, the highest of which has a view through a small window of Mounts Bay and St Michael's Mount, over the chimney pots of the city.

Gothic Temple

Temple folly in the manicured landscape gardens of Stowe

Stowe School offered The Landmark Trust a long lease on this property in 1970, whose efforts provide income to maintain this splendid example of Gothic style architecture. Built in 1741, it is one of the last additions to the garden at Stowe formed for Lord Cobham. That same year, 'Capability' Brown arrived as gardener, to begin his transformation of the landscape to create one of the finest landscape gardens in the world.

Lord Cobham decided to dedicate his new temple, designed by James Gibbs, 'to the Liberty of our Ancestors', for which the Gothic style was deemed appropriate. Triangular in plan, with castellated gables, accommodation and facilities are contained in the three pentagonal turrets with large Gothic windows, decorated with knobbly pinnacles. The rooms are all circular inside, with mounded stone pilasters and plaster vaults. The main vault of the central space is gorgeously painted with heraldry and from the first floor gallery you can start to appreciate the architectural majesty of the building. At the top of the staircase is a belvedere with stone seats offering a fine view of the landscape, now presided over by The National Trust.

The ground floor provides a kitchen in the base of one tower, and modern bath and conveniences in the second – if in rather surprising places. In between is a lounge with a view of the vaulted ceiling. Climbing the stairs encased in the third tower, you reach two double bedrooms – one in each tower, providing accommodation for four.

As might be expected in such a cavernous property, with high vaulted ceilings and solid stone walls, the effect of the heating system is slight – if any. Be prepared to wrap up well for early or late season breaks, or better still, ignore the temperature and just enjoy the amazing surroundings.

Balancing Barn

Cantilevered silver barn looking over a nature reserve

Located on a site on the edge of a Suffolk Wildlife Trust reserve, this stunning property overlooks a small lake. Although the barn is clad in reflective steel tiles, it is unobtrusively located at the end of a tree-lined driveway set back from a quiet country road. It isn't until you view the property from the side that you appreciate that while half of the 30-metre-long building is anchored to the ground, the other half juts out into the valley, with nothing but space underneath. This cantilevered construction balances the building on a concrete plinth embedded into the hillside, so although balanced, it feels solid underfoot. It looks amazing. The property is filled with practical and usable features, showing the care and attention of the Dutch design team who crafted this construction. Stylish continental lighting illuminates each of the four double, en suite, bedrooms, kitchen/diner at the anchored end, and suspended over the valley – lounge area with fireplace. All along the sides of the barn are full-height windows and in the lounge area, a glass floor. This floor deserves special mention, as it overlooks the childrens' (and adults') swing that is suspended underneath the barn.

Photos © Jack Hobhouse

House in the Clouds

Former water tank, in Merrie England village

The House in the Clouds was originally intended to provide an adequate storage capacity for a basic water supply for Thorpeness village in 1923. Faced with the difficult task of hiding a rather hideous structure, the engineering team brilliantly disguised it as a house, which from miles around seems to be a cottage lodged 70 ft up in the trees. The supporting steel structure was boarded in to provide unique living accommodation, although for many years the accommodation did not include the very top of the tower, which housed the 50,000 gallon water tank. In 1977, the use of the tank for storage was discontinued and it passed into private ownership. As befits a structure that once held near 350 tons of water, the house is very sturdily built. The many tiny windows offer good light and ventilation. Last refurbished in 2002, it provides spacious accommodation for family holidays having five bedrooms, two with double beds, three with twin beds and an additional double sofa bed. Three bathrooms, drawing room, dining room and the magnificent 'room at the top' give the finest views of Suffolk.

The five floors are connected by a total of sixty-seven stairs with four landings and five half-landings – resting seats for the less able on each landing. There is an iron spiral staircase on the fifth floor to the upper gallery.

The Pineapple

Stunning, elaborate, eccentric summerhouse

The Pineapple is an elaborate summerhouse of two storeys, built for the 4th Earl of Dunmore. Though classical and orthodox at ground level, it grows slowly into something entirely vegetable; conventional architraves put out shoots and end as prickly leaves of stone. It is an eccentric work, of undoubted genius, built of the very finest masonry. It probably began as a one-storey pavilion, dated 1761, and only grew its fruity dome after 1777 when Lord Dunmore was brought back, forcibly, from serving as Governor of Virginia. There, sailors would put a pineapple on the gatepost to announce their return home. Lord Dunmore, who was fond of a joke, announced his return more prominently.

The Pineapple presides over an immense walled garden. This, in the Scottish tradition, was built some distance from the house to take advantage of a south-facing slope. To house the gardeners, stone bothies were built on either side of the Pineapple. These make plain, unassuming rooms to stay in, although you have to go outside to get from one part to the other.

The Pineapple and its surroundings are owned by the National Trust for Scotland. The Landmark Trust took on the lease in 1973 and restored all the buildings and the walled garden, now open to the public. At the back, where the ground level is higher, there is a private garden for guests, with steps leading into the elegant room inside the Pineapple itself.

THE BEAUMONT
HOTEL

The Gormley suite of The Beaumont hotel

A spectacular room/work of art in a luxury hotel

The owners of the magnificent Beaumont hotel (with its beautiful art deco interiors) had the excellent idea, at the time of the hotel's opening, to ask designer Antony Gormley to imagine a room that would be truly out of the ordinary. The result is spectacular: on the left-hand side of the hotel, looking out from the entrance, is an impressive sculpture made of huge stone blocks assembled in a remarkable, brutalist style depicting a seated man.

Inside, the cosy room is covered with woodwork in the purest of atmospheres.

A House for Essex

Sleeping in a spectacular work of art

Overlooking the River Stour, the House of Essex is a unique piece of art and particularly unusual accommodation. Designed by British artist Grayson Perry working with architect Charles Holland, this astonishing house is built around the fictional character of Julie Cope, an ordinary woman the artist created to pay tribute to everyone in the region who saw him grow up.

With its geometric lines and mosaic-filled rooms with whimsical decorations, House for Essex was conceived as a hint to votive chapels standing along country lanes. With two bedrooms overlooking the river, a striking green-tiled bath, bespoke furniture and a large sitting room with reproductions of tapestries depicting the life of Julie Cope, the house invites guests on a unique pilgrimage that celebrates art and the simple life of Essex.

Grotte de la Cocalière

Spending a night 50 metres underground

The Cocalière Cave offers more than just a simple visit to discover the geological wonders it houses. Here you can also enjoy an exceptional overnight experience.

Housed in a glass pyramid measuring 25 square metres and 3.5 metres high, the room is located in one of the cave's vast chambers, 50 metres below ground level. Enjoy the extraordinary surroundings and the privilege of a night spent under a vault studded with natural wonders, well protected from the 14 degrees that prevail in the cave. In the morning, you can enjoy breakfast and experience the unique panorama just like some of the greatest adventurers would - like the famous speleologist Pascal Barrier, who spent 113 days in the cave in 1992.

© Benjamin Celier

The Château du Val d'Arguenon's Tree Houses

Tree houses in exceptional trees

If magical and enchanted places exist, then the Château du Val d'Arguenon is one of them. Owned by the same family for centuries (the château was sold once, but was bought back a few years later by a relative), it is now home to a large, welcoming family whose members each participate in welcoming guests or taking care of the magnificent 50-acre grounds that are home to a large number of palm trees.

The property occupies a unique location. A narrow drive at the bend of the road from Notre-Dame de Guildo to Saint-Cast-le-Guildo leads to the château. Park your car behind the château, then walk around to admire the view of the sound and small beaches waiting to welcome you. The ever-changing light is a magnificent spectacle that you can continue to admire from your treetop bedroom or tree house terrace.

The property's beautiful trees are home to 3 tree houses. The distance between them leaves guests with the feeling that they are alone in the world, which lets them fully appreciate this little corner of heaven.

VILLA CHEMINÉE

A HOUSE SET ON A GIANT 15-METRE-HIGH CHIMNEY!

La Villa Cheminée (Chimney Villa) is an extraordinary artistic project designed by Japanese artist Tatzu Nishi for the Estuaire 2009 Nantes-Saint-Nazaire art event. This work of art eventually became permanent and it is now possible to spend the night in it. The artist installed a typical 1970s villa at the top of what clearly resembles a factory smokestack (he took his inspiration from the château de Fer, the largest fossil fuel power plant in France).

Located at the head of Ile de la Nation, the villa has an unrestricted view of the Loire estuary and the rocky Sillon de Bretagne.

The house has a well-equipped kitchen and bathroom on the bottom floor, and a bedroom with a double bed on the upper floor.

A stunning little garden surrounds the house.

The Buron of Niercombe

A timeless refuge

The Buron of Niercombe is a former cheese dairy, at an altitude of 1450 m, that you reach by taking a 4x4 on a private drive, accompanied by a mountain guide who will come to pick you up on the day of your departure. In the meantime, you'll be able to enjoy the solitude and the countryside's wild beauty – an exceptional experience. The buron is a traditional stone building with a lauze stone roof that is found in mountain pastures. Traditionally in the Auvergne region, the stockbreeders in the valley who own the pastures use them in the summer months. The burons are used to house the cheese-making equipment and to lodge the cheese-makers. Many burons have been abandoned, but some are now being used again, like that of Niercombe. The interior décor is simple, but welcoming. The furniture and flooring are made of wood, and there is a stairway leading down to the kitchen and bathroom below the main room. The water comes from the property's own springs. The Buron of Niercombe, which was built on a ledge more than 300 years ago, overlooks the Cère valley. It provided shelter to shepherds up to the 1940s, but was then left abandoned to the nature of the Monts du Cantal for over 60 years. It took 4 years of restoration work to turn it into this enchanting, timeless place.

Cadoles de la Colline du Colombier

Spectacular modernist cocoons

Iguérande's cadoles (named after the old cabins generally built of dry stone that once sheltered wine growers in Burgundy) are spectacular houses on piles, built on a hillside. One of these 3 contemporary homes is suspended in the air; the second, a terrace, fits snugly between two 100-year-old oak trees, and the third is shaded by an apple tree. Guests can live comfortably in all three, since each one is furnished with a large bed, bathroom, small kitchen and a spacious Zen-style living-room that opens onto a balcony overlooking the natural surroundings.

The bedrooms are designed like cocoons. Woven hemp covers the ceiling and walls, which seem to blend together to give an incredible effect. This 100% ecological project was conceived by Marie-Pierre and the famous Michael Troisgros, with the help of the no less famous architect Patrick Bouchain. A former adviser to French politician Jack Lang, Bouchain represented France at Venice's Architecture Biennale in 2006.

He designed the Zingaro equestrian theatre in Aubervilliers and the 'Lieu Unique' in Nantes. Here, the property is also home to an inn housed in a former stable, called 'Le Grand Couvert', but you can always go another 15km and dine at Michael Troisgros' gourmet restaurant (3 Michelin stars) in Roanne.

Le Corbusier Hotel

A unique way to spend the night in a Le Corbusier building

Almost as famous as the nearby velodrome stadium, Le Corbusier's 'Cité Radieuse' (Radiant City), classed as a historic monument, possesses a hotel on the third floor. Unknown to most of Marseille's residents, it was taken over in 2003 by a couple of architecture enthusiasts who redecorated it in the spirit of the period, by reintegrating some of the original furniture and light fixtures and having others reproduced (with the authorization of Charlotte Perriand, who was part of the team). Although the result is true to the original, many clients don't necessarily appreciate the 'master's' architecture: the corridors are long, dark and sinister, and the rather sparse décor doesn't really give it the feeling of an up-scale hotel. Situated outside of Marseille's city centre, the site will delight fans of Le Corbusier most of all.

The rest of the building, which is a veritable village in and of itself, is also open to the hotel's clients: a 40-seat cinema, fitness room and sauna, jogging lanes, children's wading pool, and a concert hall on the roof terrace.

From the restaurant's terrace (where breakfast is served), you have a glorious view of the sea and the Frioul Islands.

The Château Valmer Tree House

A tree house in a vineyard

Standing 6 m above ground in the branches of an immense 100-year-old oak tree on the Château Valmer estate, the tree house is a romantic refuge of overwhelming charm. Isolated from the rest of the château in the middle of a vineyard that covers the majority of this 19th-century estate, the tree house is probably the most beautiful of its kind in France. Only the price might disappoint some. In the summer, you can have a delicious breakfast brought right to the bedroom door. Although you can't see the ocean from the tree house, it is nevertheless nearby, barely 200m away, at the end of a gorgeous pathway lined by 100-year-old trees.

The beach itself is probably one of the most beautiful and wild beaches along the French Riviera. A few rare buildings, including the annex of the Château Valmer, with a swimming pool and restaurant, make this site a very pleasant place.

On the left, after a second beach with more buildings, a pathway begins along the coast which, after a few hours of walking, will lead you to the Saint-Tropez peninsula. Bought in 1949 by the parents of the current owners, Château Valmer was progressively turned into a 4-star hotel with 42-two rooms, a restaurant, spa, sauna and hammam.

AS

The Jean Prouvé room in the CAB foundation

Sleeping in a Jean Prouvé work of art

Opened in 2021 in Saint-Paul-de-Vence by the contemporary art collector Hubert Bonnet, the remarkable CAB foundation, which specialises in minimal and conceptual art, had the excellent idea of opening the premises to the public for overnight stays.

Among the five beautiful rooms, one in particular stands out: it consists of a dismountable house created in 1944 by the designer Jean Prouvé (1901–1984) and installed at the time in the Gérardmer region in the Vosges.

The house was adapted as a bedroom and furnished, of course, with furniture by Prouvé, but also by Pierre Jeanneret, George Nakashima and Charlotte Perriand.

For fans of design and architecture, this is a unique experience.

Called the 6x6 house because of its size (6 metres by 6 metres, or 36 square metres), the dismountable house was designed to meet the needs of reconstruction after the Second World War, particularly in Alsace-Lorraine. Prouvé designed affordable, prefabricated, standardised elements to meet massive demand.

Note that there is also a Jean Prouvé room at Château La Coste, near Aix, but the prices are much higher and the atmosphere less intimate.

The Citerne-Lit

Sleeping in a work of art on the route to Santiago de Compostela

Designed by Fred Sancère and Encore Heureux architects, the Citerne-Lit (tank cistern bedroom) is unusual accommodation and one of the seven art-refuge works of a project called Fenêtres sur le paysage ('Windows overlooking the landscape'). Launched by the Derrière le Hublot collective, this project offers an open-air artistic journey following the GR65 walking route to Santiago de Compostela.

The Citerne-Lit invites visitors to immerse themselves in the world of the countryside. The room itself is a work of art. It is built on the model of an agricultural water tank and provides a cosy nest in which to discover all the charms a night in the middle of nature can offer.

The tank houses a large and comfortable bed, and the rest of the space is optimised in a way reminiscent of space capsules, right down to the spartan facilities on the site (dry toilets and solar shower). The local breakfast will bring the stay to a pleasant conclusion, before heading to one of the other art refuges in the project, such as La Chambre d'Or in Golinhac or Vivre Seule in Livinhac-Le-Haut, both in the Aveyron.

The Best of Home suite in Martin's Patershof hotel

Sleeping in an old church

In 2009, Martin's hotels moved into the former church of the Friars Minor. Located in the centre of Mechelen, 20 minutes from the centre of Brussels and 10 minutes from Zaventem international airport, the church was built in 1863 and has managed to keep the structure and certain architectural details of its original neo-Gothic style. Of the 79 rooms, the Best of Home suite is the one that has best preserved the impressive original atmosphere with its stained-glass windows and vaults.

Hotel Inntel Zaandam

Madcap collection of classic Dutch building façades

One look at the twelve-storey Hotel Inntel Zaandam will astound you.

Like a collection of different houses, assembled on top and alongside each other in a life-size jigsaw, you'll simply be amazed – and undoubtedly amused.

Chief Architect Wilfried van Winden of WAM, the director of the Delft-based bureau, modestly suggests that he didn't set out to shock. Instead, his wish was to avoid the bland, impersonal approach of traditional hotels, and create something more like a home-from-home, with façades based on traditional Zaanstad houses: 'From a stately notary's dwelling,' he quotes, 'to workers cottages.'

Inside, rooms retain their personal feel, themed according to traditional elements of Zaandam's heritage and manufacturing past. The Zaanstad region has a long tradition of rich aromas and rooms are decorated with wall-sized enlargements of advertisements for Zaandam-manufactured chocolate, cheese, mustard and biscuits, as well as black and white photos from the bygone industrial past of the town.

Marqués de Riscal

A stunning Gehry-designed hotel

A roofline of shimmering ribbons of pink, gold and silver titanium, the hotel Marqués de Riscal in the northern Spanish town of Elciego echoes the Gehry Associates trademark architecture found in the Guggenheim Bilbao and Bridge of Life building in Panama.

The main Gehry-designed hotel has forty-three rooms and is stunning in

every respect, both externally and internally, with designer furniture and hi-tech gadgets. There are also a number of more traditional, utilitarian rooms in an annex, connected to Hotel Marqués de Riscal by a bridge, where the spa and pool are located. Although the annex rooms have views of the vineyard and artistic furnishings, they lack the outrageous charm of the main building.

There are two restaurants in the hotel: '1860' and the more formal Marqués de Riscal restaurant which is closed on Mondays. While there have been mixed reviews for the more formal restaurant, the executive chef is the Michelin-starred Francis Paniego, so an average meal is unlikely and the wines will most certainly be exceptional.

The spa itself is worthy of mention for it provides wine therapy treatments using products made from grape extracts, created exclusively by Caudalie Vinothérapie. It has received many awards for the treatments and venue.

© David Mapletoft

Hotel Puerta América Madrid

Every floor a different design adventure

With twelve floors and communal spaces providing a unique style designed by nineteen design agencies, your choice of room is critical at Hotel Puerta América. Thankfully the front-desk staff anticipate guests changing rooms. A menu of design choices for the different floors is provided at check-in and you are recommended to study closely, or to review the website in advance. Some floors are a triumph of style over substance and there are stories of guests whose frustration in trying to dim the walls or use hi-tech appliances forced them to change rooms. Although floors have a similar layout, when you leave the elevator on each floor you feel in altogether different worlds – from futuristic red plastic to black marble through to traditional leather and wood. Examples include the first floor by Zaha Hadid, where everything seems to come out from the wall. The bathroom is a single structure from floor to ceiling, which changes colour according to the room. Most frustratingly, the waste basket is a challenge for guests because it's not so easy to find. Or you can just drop your rubbish on the floor ... The eighth floor by Kathryn Findlay, 'Light in Motion', intends to suggest a feminine touch. Refusing to consider walls or doors, Findlay provided for sweeping white curtains that separate the bathroom from the room. The entire room is white and forms a single space.

Patience is required on the ninth floor with Richard Gluckman's 'Boxes of Colours' concept as you need to look for everything, all hidden in boxes. The biggest box, in the middle of the room, houses the TV. In the bathroom, the first thing you see when you enter is a large glass box containing the shower, with a sliding door separating it from the bedroom and a white metal curtain. A raw industrial look contrasts with back-lit illumination, so don't forget to ask how to turn off the lights otherwise you'll struggle to get to sleep.

With every floor a different artistic design, this hotel challenges the senses in an architectural assault course of design.

ano
1939
HOTEL
CIRC HOTEL RALUY

Circo Museo Raluy

Sleep over and enjoy the greatest show on Earth!

For all children great and small … Come in, look around and above all settle in for a comfortable stay in one of the most traditional Spanish circuses!

Since 2010, the Raluy circus museum has invited guests to stay in its 'Hotel on wheels', a wooden gypsy caravan from the early twentieth century that gives you a glimpse into the world of the circus. To be exact, let yourself be transported by the magic of this traditional circus, where the true artists aren't the animals but the tightrope walkers, knife throwers and clowns.

The Raluy circus is the ideal place to immerse yourself in this life of travel and to realise what a life dedicated to entertainment means. Winner of the National Circus Award in 1996 (given by the Ministry of Education and Culture) and of the Creu de Sant Jordi Award in 2006 (awarded by the Autonomous Government of Catalonia), Raluy is not just a circus, it's also a museum – a fragment of itinerant history, as illustrated by the wooden caravans and wagons of various origins: Romania, Czech Republic, England and Germany. These are genuine works of art that Luis and Carlos Raluy, brothers and owners of the circus, have restored and adapted to our era, while carefully respecting their original nineteenth- and twentieth-century appearance.

Staying in one of these caravans undoubtedly gives you the feeling of belonging to the forty-strong group who make up the extended Raluy family. It's a unique experience you won't easily forget. Indeed, circus fans and the curious-minded will all discover what a day in the life of these performers is like: dare to serve as a target for Silvano, the knife thrower; help Steacy the tightrope walker prepare her freestanding ladder routine; or watch Sandro the clown as he applies his make-up backstage. Enjoy it all without giving up the comfort of the 1939 showman caravan, where all guests stay. Spending a night here is like travelling back in time and rediscovering the ambiance of legendary circuses.

Photos © Thomas Jonglez

Palace Hotel Do Bussaco

Those who dared cut down a tree were excommunicated!

North of Coimbra, in the heart of Bussaco National Forest, stands the Palace Hotel do Bussaco, almost like a mirage. Built in 1885 for the last Portuguese kings, the hotel is a genuine romantic folly inspired by Neuschwanstein Castle, which was built for the Bavarian Ludwig II, a cousin of the King of Portugal.

This sumptuous palace seems to rise out of a fairy tale, as it is surrounded by a mysterious botanic garden dotted with gigantic trees, chapels, monasteries, lakes, belvederes and fountains of crystal-clear water.

It all began in 1628 when Dom João Melo, the count bishop of Coimbra, sent a small group of discalced Carmelite friars to the region to found a place where they could withdraw from the world and build a monastery to devote their lives to prayer and contemplation. The Carmelites also planted many trees, such as the 30 m (100 ft) cedar that has watched the centuries go by since 1644. In 1643, Pope Urban VIII issued a Papal bull to protect these 250 hectares (600 acres) of greenery: anyone who dared cut down a tree would be excommunicated!

The adventure of this Neo-Manueline style hotel began in 1917 when the owner, Alexander de Almeida, restored the abandoned castle and transformed it into a luxury hotel. He kept the original elements relating to the royal family – paintings, frescoes, azulejo panels and furniture – which allow guests to live like royalty for the duration of their stay. The artworks that decorate the hotel are one of the main points of interest for historians and art lovers. On the hotel's walls are rare works illustrating scenes from Portugal's history, such as the Battle of Bussaco, where Wellington defeated Napoleon in 1810, as well as scenes from *The Lusiads*, the epic poem by Portuguese writer Luis de Camões. The azulejos, marvellous sculpted ceilings and stone arches will certainly make a strong impression on art lovers, too.

Villa Crespi

A touch of magic

Located on the superb Lake Orta, the Villa Crespi is a jewel of Moorish architecture in the heart of the Italian lakes region, about an hour's drive north of Milan. The villa also houses a very reputable restaurant (justly so as it has two Michelin stars) that contributes to the touch of magic you feel when you arrive at this hotel. The only disadvantages are that the villa isn't directly on the lakefront, contrary to what the hotel's website might suggest. Indeed, a road (and a car park) that can be noisy in high season separates the villa from the lake. In addition, the rather charming village of Orta isn't as close as you might think – a 15-minute walk away.

Finally, if possible, opt for one of the superb suites as some visitors have been disappointed by the standard rooms.

The villa was built in 1879 for Cristoforo Benigno Crespi, a cotton manufacturer who was so impressed by a trip to Baghdad that he decided to build his own oriental-style palace. In the 1930s, Villa Crespi welcomed King Umberto di Savoia, among other VIPs, and, in the late 1980s, after a time as a spiritual centre, it was converted into a luxury hotel by the current owners.

© Francesca Pagliai

© Francesca Pagliai

© Francesca Pagliai

Atelier sul Mare

Hotel-museum of modern art

The creation of Antonio Presti, who is quite a character, Atelier sul Mare is more than a hotel. Located halfway between Palermo and Messina, it's well worth a trip even if it's not the height of luxury.

When planning your trip, don't rely on the hotel website, which doesn't do justice to the place. Although the road you can see between the hotel and the beach does exist, it turns into a cul-de-sac after a short distance and is little used. On the other hand, the view is sublime: the water comes almost up to the windows and the Aeolian Islands form a magnificent and mysterious background.

The tone of the hotel is set at the entrance: Atelier sul Mare is totally given over to modern art. In contrast to many establishments calling themselves art hotels, here the word 'art' is not taken in vain: each room has actually been designed by a different artist.

Of the forty rooms in the hotel, thirteen have been designed by modern artists. We particularly recommend the 'Prophet's Room', in homage to Pier Paolo Pasolini (by Dario Bellezza, Adele Cambria, Antonio Presti), 'Trinacria' (by Maurizio Staccioli) with its immense triangular bed, and 'Sigismond's Tower' (by Raoul Ruiz), in which the roof can be opened manually to let you sleep under the stars, spread-eagled on a vast round bed installed in the depths of a cylinder.

It should also be noted that Antonio Presti, in accordance with his social conscience, wanted to give the place a democratic character and make it accessible to the less well-off. So he has deliberately kept prices low (from €70 per person per night) and it's not unknown for him to offer one or two nights' hospitality to passing artists.

The Presidential Suite at the Principe di Savoia Hotel

Possibly the most beautiful hotel room in the world

Built in 1896, the Principe di Savoia is one of the most beautiful hotels in Milan, Italy and the world. It also has something other internationally renowned palaces do not: its exceptional presidential suite, which is considered by many to be the most beautiful hotel room in the world.

The suite is 500 square metres, has three bedrooms, several fireplaces (in perfect working condition). But, above all, it has a fabulous, private, Pompeian-style swimming pool with mosaic floors and hand-painted frescoes.

The suite also has a private spa with hammam and sauna, a large terrace on the tenth floor of the hotel and a private dining room.

Villa Médicis

Spend a night in the most beautiful villa in Rome

It's one of Rome's most amazing secrets. For several years now, the exquisite Villa Medici has offered insiders the privilege of staying in four of the villa's historic suites – the erstwhile apartments of the Medici family.

And when we say privilege, we really mean it: after dinner, as you enter the villa through the small door cut into the large central doorway, you immediately feel you're experiencing something exceptional. In the silence of the night, go up the villa's wide marble stairs to the level of the famous gardens, which spread out before you ...

The four rooms (some 70 square metres – each!) feature 16th-century frescoes by Jacopo Zucchi and period coffered ceilings. They either offer views of the marvellous gardens or 180° panoramas of Rome. One suite even has a grand piano.

N.B: These rooms don't come with luxury-hotel amenities or services: the bathrooms are basic (though there are bathtubs, at least), there's no elevator or staff to carry your luggage, and breakfast isn't served (a problem easily solved by popping over to the nearby Caffè Colbert).

A NAPOLEON LE GRAND
LES ARTS RECONNAISSANS

Hotel Ještěd

Amazing view in award-winning architectural design

From the middle of the nineteenth century Ještěd has welcomed walkers with a refreshment stop, however when the lookout tower caught fire in 1963 the opportunity to build something more spectacular was recognized. For three years designs were considered on the theme of a TV transmission tower, separate restaurant with small hotel. However, architect Karel Hubáček entered with a radical design that combined all these, to universal acclaim. The mountain-top location demanded the use of new construction methods and materials as the TV transmitter antennas needed to be enclosed within the structure to cope with the severe climatic conditions.

In 1969, the architectural solution was awarded the world-renowned Perret Prize, and in 2000 it was awarded the title of Best Czech Building of the twentieth century.

REIFEN
BENZIN
SHELL
53

CARWASH
W 108-280 S

V8 Hotel

Zeppelin airfield buildings converted to a motor-themed hotel

The four-star-rated V8 Hotel is part of the Meilenwerk complex on the old Zeppelin airfield near Böblingen. Partnered by the Porsche Museum and Mercedes Benz, car enthusiasts, collectors and restoration specialists gather together to enjoy heritage motor vehicles on display in the Legend Hall of the main event building. Collectors of classic cars may even park their car in glass viewing boxes, so that others can see the repair and servicing taking place.

The V8 Hotel itself occupies the original Bauhaus-style (1928) airport hotel building, now completely restored and updated as a listed building in its own right.

The standard rooms have some great wall photography but the theme rooms really take the automotive element to a new level. Perhaps you wish for the luxury of sleeping in a converted white Mercedes bed – bright and polished from the carwash? Maybe airbrushed custom paintwork and chrome is more your style in the Tuning bedroom? Or the 53 Beetle Herbie parked up as a bed in the Petrol Station room?

A Cadillac bed and artwork themed around the drive-in cinemas of the 50s and 60s, or a room themed for the outdoors, in V8 Camp?

While everyone will have a favourite, the Morris Minor car bed in the Workshop room – complete with mechanic under the car – deserves special mention. Your bed is hoisted on lifting jacks, and your bedside table is a drum of oil. A mechanic's workbench is your writing desk.

Rogner Bad Blumau

Spa hotel designed by eccentric Austrian artist Hundertwasser, with grass-covered roofs and rainbow façades

Inaugurated in 2000, Rogner Bad Blumau has a simply amazing eclectic design with the grass-covered roof of the main buildings following the profile of the rolling hills.

Some of the rooms are underground, with windows facing lit courtyards, while others follow the rolling landscape. A spa is at the centre of the complex, with an award-winning gourmet restaurant among the facilities. The spa has a variety of saunas and health facilities and offers a number of wellness programmes. The hot springs also provide heat and generate power for the resort.

Although the rooms are in differently themed areas, they provide a similar level of guest comfort, room service and en suite facilities. Inside, you could easily be in a well furnished four-star hotel. Outside, however, the story is dramatically different and the views are more in keeping with how you expect a hotel will look on the moon, or in a fantasy world – such is the patchwork of coloured tiles, grass and oddly positioned windows in the overall design.

Hundertwasser's artistic vision shares common themes, bright colours, organic forms, strong individualism, and a rejection of the straight line. Calling straight lines 'the devil's tools', his architectural work is comparable to Antoni Gaudí. His work has been used for flags, stamps, coins, posters, schools, churches and, most impressively, a public toilet in his adopted home of New Zealand; no matter where he went in the world, his watch was always set to New Zealand time.

Almdorf Seinerzeit tree house

A love nest facing the valley

Located 30 minutes from Villach, Almdorf Seinerzeit is a small paradise of a dozen or so chalets, each of which has two or three bedrooms. Here, you can rent an entire lodge or chalet, not just one room. All are elegantly designed and decorated (nothing flashy, just authentic wood and stone), but one chalet stands out: it has an additional little cabin set up in a tree facing the valley.

The cabin, connected by a drawbridge which, once drawn up, leaves you completely cut off from the world, is equipped with all modern comforts despite its small size. You'll just have to decide at which temperature to set the heating so you're not too hot or too cold to fully admire the beautiful view of the valley through the large bay window. Candles and matches are left at your disposal to create the perfect romantic setting. In addition to a traditional restaurant, Almdorf also has an astonishing and delightful hut that claims to be 'the smallest restaurant in the world'. This charming site allows a maximum of four people to dine facing the valley in an atmosphere that is quite enchanting thanks to the wood fire that the chef uses from time to time to prepare the meal (the rest of the time, you'll be alone in the tranquil hut).

To better appreciate the experience, before dinner we suggest trying the mountain herbal bath at the hotel spa (if you can stand water at more than 40 °C / 105 °F). In an extremely warm atmosphere (the decoction of herbs is brought to a near boil in a copper cauldron set over a wood fire in a huge stone fireplace), you rest on a bed of straw to relax as you regain your spirits.

Whitepod Eco-Luxury Hotel

Hi-tech igloos in a Swiss eco resort

Whitepod is the creation of Swiss-born Sofia de Meyer, who wanted a high-tech solution to the challenge of creating a different, eco-friendly way of catching up with yourself in the natural beauty of the Swiss Alps.

Now in its fifth year, the resort has left little mark on the environment, but made a great mark in ecotourism – winning the Responsible Tourism Award for Innovation.

The fifteen geodesic dome pods that make up Whitepod have been equipped with traditional furnishings and a simple wood-burning stove that keeps you comfortably warm. The pods are lit by lanterns and the only electricity is in the main chalet a 3 or 4 minutes' walk away. Covered with white canvas in the winter and green in the summer, they blend perfectly into the surrounding landscape. The pods themselves are built on wooden platforms, so they can be moved easily. The main chalet houses the dining and spa facilities as well as the bathrooms, although the larger pavilion pods have en suite facilities.

The view of the mountains opposite, from the large bedroom window of the pod, is stunning, even more so when the sunlight reflects off the snow to wake you up in the morning. No need for an alarm clock here. After time on the private ski run with three lifts and 7 km (4 miles) of piste, or a traditional snow-shoe randonnée (ramble) in the nearby forests, you sleep soundly and wake early – but refreshed. Perhaps it is the clear mountain air or the fondue of the previous night, but you seem to have energy that was lacking when you arrived. This outdoor effort also builds up an appetite and the resident chef provides two nightly menus, one with traditionally hearty Swiss mountain food such as raclette and fondue, the other with lighter dishes using locally sourced ingredients. Such is the integration with the community, that Whitepod even runs a small grocery store for villagers.

Iglu-Dorf

Sleep in an artist igloo or build your own!

Adrian Günter built his first igloo in 1996, to better enjoy the mountain and first powder snow of the day. Following an avalanche of interest from friends wanting to sample an igloo night, he increased the number of igloos and opened the 'small world in white' in 2004, with six villages across Andorra, Switzerland and Germany now accepting guests.

Moving 3,000 tons of snow every December to build each village, Adrian invites artists to craft sculptures inside each village. With only an ice pick, motor saw and shovel, artists produce seals, arctic wolves, polar bears and whales as well as swirling designs and patterns illuminated by candlelight to overlook the guests from the walls.

The villages are open from Christmas Day to the beginning of April each year, snow conditions permitting. With 10,000 visitors in 2010, all ages have enjoyed the cosy hospitality of an expedition sleeping bag and sheepskin rug, from the youngest 19-month-old baby to an 83-year-old lady guest.

A variety of igloo options are available in the different villages, from standard and group igloos to 'Romantic' suites with private whirlpool or sauna. The team have even built a church, including an altar and baptismal font for a wedding party. Every village is equipped with a large igloo hotel lobby and bar where the evening meal of cheese fondue and mulled wine is served. The top-range 'Romantic-plus' igloos even include their own toilet.

II
BOTVID

Kolarbyn

Sleep in a 'camouflage' hut in the woods, with no electricity

Kolarbyn consists of twelve little forest huts located by the beautiful Lake Skärsjön. Known as Sweden's most primitive hotel, the huts have no electricity and the dark evenings are lit by candles or traditional oil lamps. Each hut provides two berths with sheepskin rugs to cushion your slumber. You're kept warm by a wood heater, and your first task is to gather and chop enough wood for your cooking and heating needs.

During the week guests bring food to cook themselves at one of several fireplaces – one even has a view over the lake. The nearest supermarket is 3 km away at Skinnskatteberg, and pans and cutlery are available in the storehouse. At weekends, food can be provided for those making a reservation in advance.

There is also a sauna to chop wood for, although as washing facilities are limited to a stream, you are encouraged to be brave enough to cool down with a dip in the nearby lake.

Toilets are in natural outhouses which, though rustic, serve their purpose adequately, as was the normal practice for centuries!

Treehotel

Tree houses in a woodland setting

This stunning treetop accommodation in Harads in northern Sweden was designed with the help of six well-known designers and architects, who turned their ideas into unique tree houses, created in harmony with nature and their ecological values.

All the tree houses are sited in pine trees between 4–6 m (13–20 ft) from the ground. The rooms can be accessed either by a ramp or sturdy steps. One of them has an electric, retractable stepladder.

They each have their own living and sleeping areas with between two and four beds. In addition there is a sauna and a relaxing room seating twelve guests comfortably. This is the first tree hotel with a sauna!

Photos ©Peter Lundstrom, WDO

Jumbo Stay

Sleep in the cockpit of a 747

This 1976 vintage jumbo jet guarantees a memorable night for guests in a variety of room options, from shared low-cost dormitories to a couple of luxury suites, one in the cockpit and the other in the tail.

The dormitory rooms have single, twin, three-bed and four-bed combinations with shared shower and toilet in the corridor. They're comfortable and clean and perfect for those with early flights at the airport.

The luxury suites are much more of a treat and the converted cockpit provides a view of the airport taxiway.

You're guaranteed a unique and outstanding experience for all budgets.

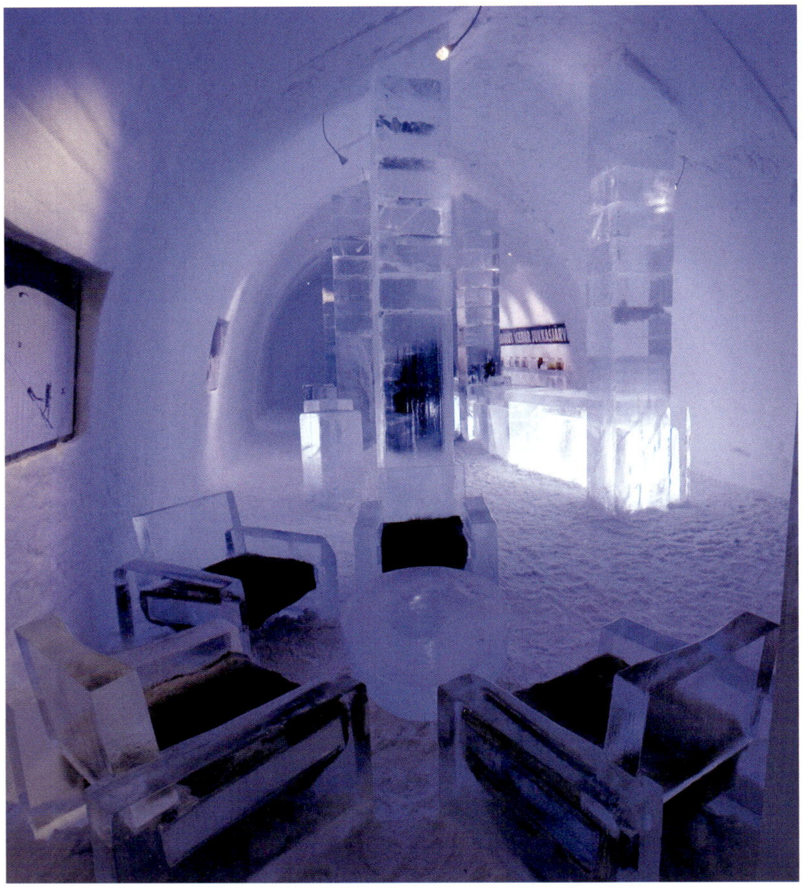

ICEHOTEL

SLEEP AT −5 °C IN AN EPHEMERAL WORK OF ART

Although the Icehotel has become a classic of the unexpected and has featured in most of the world's magazines (Kate Moss and Naomi Campbell have been photographed here), it's still an undefinable place that will satisfy the most curious among you – and the least sensitive to the cold!

The peculiar feature of this hotel, first created in the early 1990s, is that it is (re)built every year at the beginning of winter with the frozen water of the nearby river, and it melts every spring. The cycle is complete: the river water turns to ice and then returns naturally to the river some six months later...

The Icehotel offers two types of accommodation: bedrooms or suites. In both cases you sleep on a block of ice covered with an insulating sheet and reindeer skins and the ambient temperature is around −5 °C. As the suites are all designed by different artists, if you have the means don't hesitate to book one of them; the impression of sleeping in an actual work of art is quite extraordinary.

The hotel also offers the famous and indispensable Icebar, open to non-residents, as well as an ice chapel sought out by some couples as a likely venue to get married. Although all this seems idyllic on paper, the sleeping bags are not always up to the task: if you want to avoid being wakened around 6 in the morning feeling cold, bring your own severe-weather sleeping bag. Also bring your warmest clothes, even if you'll probably wear the jumpsuit that the hotel kindly hands out to guests on arrival.

Finally, beware of the 'warm rooms': they're comfortable but quite expensive and have no bathtub.

Of the two restaurants near the hotel, we strongly recommend the one furthest away: it is in a much more charming setting and the walk is very pleasant (see following page on aurora borealis).

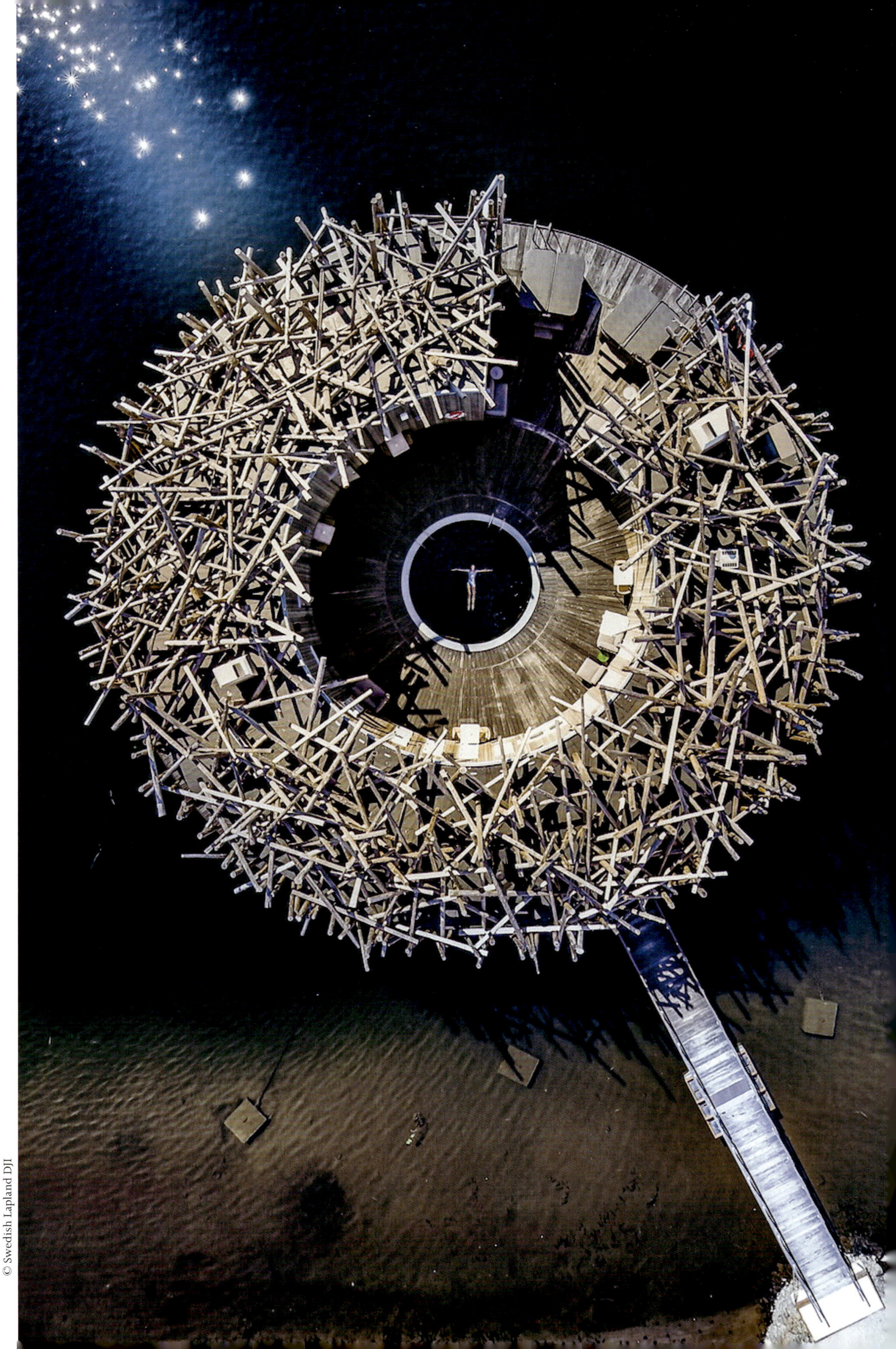

Arctic Bath

Scandinavian designs in the heart of Swedish Lapland

Arctic Bath is in the heart of Swedish Lapland, in the very north of the country, in a magnificent setting not far from the Arctic Circle. It is a unique hotel open all year, in winter for cross-country skiing, dog sledding, snowmobiling and watching the northern lights, and in summer for exploring the surrounding forests, kayaking or diving into the river for a swim under the midnight sun.

In addition to the many activities, the hotel offers a high-quality restaurant, a beautifully designed circular spa and 12 luxurious, minimally designed rooms overlooking the water or the banks of the Lule River.

The unique Tree Hotel (see p. 113) is only a few minutes' drive away.

© Malin Saxcom

© Swedish Lapland

© Bilder

© Viggo Lundberg

© Norrland

© Pasquale Basecotto

© AlexAndJames

Manta Resort Underwater room

Room service by boat and a whole new meaning to 'sea view'

The Manta Resort, 1.5 hours north of the airport on Pemba Island (30 minutes north of Zanzibar by plane), is a beautiful hotel with the unique feature of an exceptional underwater room about 200 metres from the shore.

The 'Underwater Room' is designed on three levels: a roof terrace for sunbathing or star-gazing (perfect for disconnecting from everything), a lounge at water level (with shower, toilet and fridge) and the room itself, four metres underwater, with 360-degree panoramic windows. The fish are particularly numerous at sunrise and at night, attracted by the lighting.

Dinner and breakfast are brought on site by boat.

It is a rare place offering a unique experience to disconnect from the world in a magical setting.

BEACH HOUSE

The Grand Daddy

Airstream caravans on hotel roof

Right in the centre of Cape Town, the roof of the Grand Daddy Hotel has been converted into an Airstream Penthouse Park with seven vintage Airstream caravans.

Decorated by local artists, each Airstream is unique: 'Goldilocks and the Three Bears' comes complete with a bear suit and Goldilocks outfit, and tiny cups and saucers; 'The Ballad of John & Yoko' has a bed taking up three-quarters of the trailer; and 'Love of Lace' offers lingerie decoratively framed to inspire boudoir thoughts. Even the most spacious Airstream suite, 'Moontides', has been given the full designer treatment, with an interior in a dreamy silver and blue combination.

A vintage elevator takes you to the rooftop, where you can enjoy the view while sipping a cocktail from the Sky Bar or watching a film at the Pink Flamingo rooftop cinema.

The Sky Suite of the Kaggakamma Hotel

A luxury room in the wilderness

About 3.5 hours north of Cape Town, on the edge of the magnificent Cederberg Mountains, the Kaggakamma Hotel is set amid magnificent wilderness and a raw landscape. To make the most of it, you should book the Sky Suite. Located 3 km from the main building at the foot of a huge rock, it offers fantastic privacy in the middle of nature.

You will sleep with your head in the stars, without a roof, without a mosquito net (there are no mosquitoes there). It feels like landing on Earth for the first time.

A few steps away, a natural swimming pool allows you to refresh yourself. There is also an outdoor shower and a free-standing bathtub to warm up at the end of the day, before spending some enjoyable time in front of a wood fire, not far from your bed ...

Kruger Shalati

A spectacular hotel in a train on a bridge

The Kruger Shalati, at the gateway to the beautiful Kruger National Park, is a spectacular hotel of 24 railway carriages parked in the middle of a bridge over the Sabie River in the heart of the wilderness. In the 1920s, the railway line was the only way to access the park.

Each room occupies an entire railway carriage in an art deco style. In addition to the 24 wagons (plus a swimming pool and lounge) on the bridge, the hotel also has a few rooms, a reception, another swimming pool and a restaurant by the river. Accommodation rates include two safaris to the surrounding area, which is considered one of the best places in the whole park to see lions.

It is one of a kind.

Hippo Point Wildlife Sanctuary

Pagoda folly in the middle of a wildlife sanctuary

This delicate 40 m Kenyan cypress-clad pagoda stands 12 m wide at its base and offers four double rooms and a single inside the nine-storey construction. Nestling within the surrounding yellow acacia 'fever' trees that surround much of Lake Naivasha, the design is completely accepted by wildlife, fooling short-sighted hippos to think that the tower is part and parcel of the landscape, a towering yellow acacia itself. It offers close-up views of monkeys, birds, giraffe, impala, zebra and of course the hippos that give the place its name. Completed in 1993, Dodo's tower is the eccentric folly of Dodo Cunningham-Reid, who wanted to build something special in Kenya.

Originally planned as a weekend escape for Dodo and husband Michael when visiting their 250 hectare Nderit estate, there is impressive attention to detail. The top of the tower provides a 360 degree observation lookout, while a floor below is a minaret-style meditation room, furnished with big cushions and a surround view. The middle tiers of the tower offer bedrooms with crisp Russian linens and covered verandas. Down spiral stairs you reach a mahogany-panelled lounge and drawing room, spectacularly original yet luxuriously functional.

Welcoming guests for an overnight stay or personalized rental, the tower and its staff cater for guests to enjoy their day at a leisurely pace. Perhaps breakfast on the veranda, hippo-watching while sipping English tea and freshly squeezed juices, or maybe a walk among the animals of the wildlife sanctuary itself. An afternoon might be spent on the lake in the beautiful teak Riva motorboat before a candle-lit gourmet dinner using foods from their on-site organic garden or fresh from the nearby farms. Such is the harmonious way that Hippo Point Tower integrates guest activities with the wildlife of the estate, you could perhaps forget that the 500 wallowing hippos peacefully waggling their ears in the lake are each two tons of wild animal. Given the protection that the estate affords the animals, they are very relaxed in human company and respectful of the guest presence, allowing a close-up experience of them in their natural habitat that is as unique as it is rewarding. A magical place.

Loisaba Star Bed

Star Beds for waterhole views and star gazing

Loisaba Wilderness camp is a 61,000-acre (25,000-hectare) private ranch and game sanctuary where guests can see Africa's wildlife in the untamed bush, as it was before fences were erected and game-park rules applied. Not only is it outstandingly beautiful, it's also a working cattle farm – managed in cooperation with the Samburu and Maasai tribesmen, who have defended this land for generations. Whether you're sleeping in the main Lodge, the House or the Cottage, or on the Star Beds, you'll enjoy an abundance of wildlife and amazing vistas.

The rooms in the Lodge, Cottage and House are beautifully furnished, all with furniture handmade at Loisaba. The Lodge has a swimming pool, tennis court, bocce court and croquet lawn, and a spa offering massage and beauty treatments. The highlight is a romantic open-air bubble bath overlooking the unspoilt Karissia Hills.

The fantastic Star Beds are strongly recommended: they allow you to gaze up at a starry sky from the comfort of your own bed.

Giraffe Manor

A colonial house where you can have lunch with giraffes

Built in the 1930s in a delightful colonial style in the heart of the stylish neighbourhood of Langata, south of Nairobi (about 45 minutes by taxi from the two Nairobi airports), Giraffe Manor is exceptional. It has magnificent rooms, perfectly groomed gardens (6 hectares in the middle of a 60-hectare forest) and a perfectly preserved, chic English colonial atmosphere.

But Giraffe Manor, as its name suggests, has a unique attraction: it is possible to approach giraffes, and warthogs, that live on the property.

You can feed a giraffe that pops its head into the breakfast room or feed it from the terrace of your room. You will also be surprised to brush up against warthogs (think Pumbaa in *The Lion King*) and discover they are not at all dangerous, contrary to what their appearance suggests.

Very expensive but exceptional.

Niassam Hills Lodge

Rooms in a baobab tree

Niassam Hills Lodge is extraordinary, in the real sense of the word. In an isolated area of Senegal on the remarkable Siné Saloum delta, it is particularly well located facing a lagoon and an island covered in magnificent baobabs.

The site alone is worth a visit: although the official journey time from Dakar is 3½ hours, it frequently takes as long as 5 or 6 hours, depending on the state of your vehicle and the usually horrendous traffic out of Dakar, notably when nearing Rusfique, the nightmare of all Senegalese drivers. You may after all be pleased about your plane's arrival time (most European flights land in the middle of the night), as it means you'll miss all the traffic jams.

The yellow and black taxis that you'll find at the airport are sometimes in a dreadful state. Even though these shortcomings are offset by the legendary kindness (the justly famous *teranga*) of the Senegalese, we nevertheless advise you to arrange for a car to be sent from the lodge.

The hotel itself consists of thirteen rooms: four perched in the baobab trees and four on stilts, while the others are more classic and thus less interesting. The decor of the baobab and stilt rooms is a great success: wood, traditional furniture, mosquito net. The setting is enchanting: whether viewed from a hammock on one of the balconies outside a baobab room, or from an armchair on the little terrace of one of the rooms on stilts looking directly out over the water, the landscape is splendid and the atmosphere conducive to meditative daydreaming. If they're available, go for the two rooms on stilts located on the little private island, accessible by means of walkways across the water ...

With plenty of *bandes dessinées* (comic strip albums) in the library, a swimming pool (not quite as satisfactory as the rest but especially suitable for children), very decent cuisine, and kayaks available, all in all you'll have a fantastic stay here.

ATLANTIS, THE PALM

SLEEP IN A GIANT AQUARIUM!

Located at the end of the manmade The Palm island in Dubai, the 'Atlantis, the Palm' Hotel, built to the same design as the one in the Bahamas, is a giant resort of over 1,500 rooms.

Among the myriad guest rooms and activities that you'd expect from this type of establishment, the two Underwater Suites – Neptune and Poseidon – are particularly unusual: on 165 m2 (1,776 sq. ft) spread out over three floors, they offer the fantastic possibility of sleeping (as well as taking your bath) right in front of the hotel's giant Lost Chambers Aquarium, containing around 65,000 fish and sea mammals.

Even if the huge hammerhead shark is no longer around, there are still an uncountable number of manta rays. The show is truly impressive and, whether from your bed or your bathtub, you'll never tire of admiring the fishy ballet!

It's also possible to take a dip in the aquarium itself (the price – a hefty one – must be confirmed with the hotel in advance). Through the glass pane that separates the aquarium from your suite, you could even propose to your beloved – who will, of course, have remained sagely waiting inside the room ...

Ulpotha Yoga & Ayurveda Retreat

A magical place

Ulpotha is a magical place, hidden deep in the heart of Sri Lanka. Here you can practise yoga and meditation, receive Ayurvedic treatments or just come to relax and unwind or meet friends. The village nestles in a peaceful, lush natural environment, on the shores of a superb lake (where you can take a swim) encircled by mountains.

You can choose between a classic cabin open to the elements, a tree house (for two) or a romantic lakeside house on stilts.

For a deeper experience, you can even organise a retreat in a cave situated a few hundred metres above the lake and have your food delivered every day … Perfect for a few days far from the madding crowd!

Taprobane Island

A colonial dream

At 50 m from Weligama Bay on the southern coast of Sri Lanka (access by foot during low tide or by getting a bit wet at high tide), a 4-hour drive from Colombo and a 30-minute drive from Galle, the private island of Taprobane is a veritable dream come true. Built for the Count of Mauny-Talvande, the descendant of one of Napoleon's generals, this 1930s octagonal house in pure Colonial style and influenced by Italian architect Palladio was the home of American author Paul Bowles, and then that of the son of Balthus, the artist, before being turned into a rental property.

Although it isn't particularly luxurious, which helps keep the prices reasonable when fully occupied, the house is quite pleasant to live in. You can lunch or dine in a different place each day, get a massage in the luxurious gardens, or simply swim in the overflow pool (the water of which is curiously a bit chilly). The five members of the staff will cheerfully cater to all your desires.

Bring a few CDs, embrace the unique privilege of spending time in this exceptional place and live to the fullest the pleasures of inhabiting the only private island in Sri Lanka.

Photos © Justin Nicholas

The Muraka Suite of the Conrad Maldives Rangali Island Resort

A spectacular underwater suite

The Conrad Maldives Rangali Island resort has 150 luxury suites, but one room is much more remarkable than the others. The spectacular Muraka Suite is a private residence on the water with the unique feature of an underwater room 5 metres below the surface of the ocean.

With its particularly modern design, the Muraka residence is built on two levels and can accommodate nine people. There are another two rooms at water level along with everything needed for a very comfortable stay, including a dining room and private pool.

Hang Nga Guesthouse

Expressionist crazy guesthouse

Originally built as a personal project by Vietnamese architect and owner Dang Viet Nga, this organically designed guesthouse and gallery, resembling a five-storey-high banyan tree, has been open to the public since 1990. Nga's privileged upbringing as daughter of the late Truong Chinh, Viet Nam's second president, meant that the authorities took a lenient view of the outlandish design. However, it still took over 10 years for it to be recognised as 'Expressionist' and given official sanction.

There are few straight edges and rather than designing in a traditional way, using engineering drawings as plans, Nga produces paintings and asks local craftsmen to transform them into structural elements.

With bespoke furniture in each room and stone decorations of animals throughout the property, this is as much an art menagerie as a guesthouse.

Sheraton

Sheraton Huzhou Hot Spring Resort

Eye-catching, ring-shaped design

The architecture of the Sheraton Huzhou Hot Spring Resort, a kind of giant ring, is truly spectacular. Coupled with a lighting system that illuminates the hotel's facade in different colours at night, its reflection in the lake resembles a full moon.

The two towers – Crystal and Jade – that make up the 27-storey structure soar some 91 m (300 ft) above ground.

The base of the towers is equally stunning. The centrepiece is a huge lump of Persian rough jade, known as the 'Holy Jade', weighing approximately 28 tonnes. The hotel's porticoes and ceiling are inlaid with citrine, a type of jade that symbolizes wealth, while the front desk and concierge desks are decorated with Red Rose cryolite and Silk Road cryolite, evoking Huzhou's history as the starting point of the ancient Silk Road trade route.

Benesse Art House

Like a science fiction film set ...

Benesse House is an incredible place. In a setting that hovers between James Bond in *Dr No* and the TV series *The Prisoner*, your stay here is bound to be one of the best memories of your trip.

Built by the celebrated Japanese architect Tadao Ando, Benesse House opened in 1995 and has evolved constantly ever since.

In a building that serves as a museum for the modern art collection of Japanese multimillionaire Nobuko Fukutake, Tadao Ando has created a dozen or so rooms that form part of the museum itself. One great advantage is that, once the visitors have left for the day, the building is at your disposal and you can wander freely among the artworks. In fact, to reach the restaurant (featuring a painting by Basquiat) from your room, you have to pass through the museum...

Other than works worthy of any international museum (Giacometti, Jasper Johns, Sam Francis, Jackson Pollock, David Hockney...), some of the art is exhibited in the open air right down to the beach, where there is a jacuzzi... Useable at night, this faces an extraordinary desert-like volcanic island which adds to the mysterious and enigmatic nature of the place. Just so that you don't miss anything, when the tide is high swimming is a real delight.

From the different types of room on offer, the top choices are those in the 'Oval'. Access is by a little private monorail, like something out of a science fiction film, especially at night when the waning light of the carriage lamp illuminates the surroundings like the eye of a Cyclops. Once you're up there, the entrance to the famous Oval is spectacular: concealed inside the walls surrounding a small oval space, six doors lead to the bedrooms. Above, the enclosure is open to the sky, creating a real architectural work of art. From the rooms, the sea view is superb and the traditional hi-tech Japanese toilets will delight fans of technological gadgetry.

Treeful Treehouse Sustainable Resort

A night under the treetops

In the heart of the lush Yambaru National Park on the island of Okinawa in southern Japan, the Treeful Treehouse Hotel offers, as its name suggests, beautiful treehouse rooms. Unlike many establishments whose 'treehouses' are only one or two metres above the ground, Treeful Treehouse designed the rooms to sit high in the canopy.

Everything has been designed with an ecological conscience. The lawn, for example, is not mown by machines but by goats.

House of Light

Sleeping in James Turrell's work of art

In the Echigo-Tsumari region, south of Niigata and north-west of Tokyo (about 3.5 hours drive from Tokyo), the House of Light is the only work of art by the famous American artist James Turrell in which it is possible to sleep.

Inspired by Junichiro Tanizaki's book *In Praise of Shadows*, the House of Light is a traditional Japanese house where particular attention was paid to light and shadows. Its strong point is the roof, and the central part can be opened to the sky. At sunrise and sunset, you can lie on the futons of the house to admire the changing hues of the sky that blend with those of the house, in a sensory experience that borders on meditation, as Turrell intended.

€ : LESS THAN 100 € A NIGHT - €€ : 100 TO 300 € A NIGHT - €€€ : MORE THAN 300 € A NIGHT

Free Spirit Spheres 7
420 Horne Lake Rd, Qualicum Beach,
BC V9K 1Z7, Canada
info@freespiritspheres.com
freespiritspheres.com
€€

Quinta Real Zacatecas 9
Segunda de Palomares,
Zacatecas Centro,
98000 Zacatecas, Zac., Mexico
reservaciones@caminoreal.com
caminoreal.com/en/quintareal/
quinta-real-zacatecas
€€

Costa Verde 11
Puntarenas Province, Quepos,
Costa Rica
reservations@costaverde.com
costaverde.com
€€

Canopy Tower 13
Cerro Semáforo,
Avenida Omar Torrijos,Panama
contactus@canopytower.com
canopytower.com/canopy-tower/
€€

Skylodge Adventure Suites 15
Pista 224 km,Urubamba-Ollantaytambo,
Urubamba, Peru
info@naturavive.com
naturavive.com/web/skylodge-adventure-suites
€€€

Magic Mountain Hotel 19
Camino Internacional Panguipulli Neltume,
Panguipulli, Región de los Ríos, Chile
reservas@huilohuilo.com
huilohuilo.com/en
€€

The Egyptian House 21
Chapel St, Penzance TR18 4AW,
United Kingdom
bookings@landmarktrust.org.uk
landmarktrust.org.uk/search-and-book/landmark-groups/egyptian-house/#Search
€

Gothic Temple 23
Stowe, Buckingham MK18 5ED,
United Kingdom
bookings@landmarktrust.org.uk
landmarktrust.org.uk/search-and-book/properties/gothic-temple-8075/#Overview
€

Balancing Barn 29
Thorington, Halesworth IP19 9JG, United Kingdom
info@living-architecture.co.uk
living-architecture.co.uk/the-houses/balancing-barn/overview
€€€

House in the Clouds 33
12A Uplands Rd, Thorpeness, Leiston IP16 4NQ, United Kingdom
info@houseintheclouds.co.uk
houseintheclouds.co.uk
€€€

The Pineapple 35
Dunmore Park, Airth, Falkirk FK2 8LU, United Kingdom
bookings@landmarktrust.org.uk
landmarktrust.org.uk/search-and-book/properties/pineapple-10726/#Overview
€

The Beaumont Hotel 39
Brown Hart Gardens, Mayfair, London, United Kingdom
thebeaumont.com
€€€

A House for Essex 43
Black Boy Ln, Wrabness, Manningtree CO11 2TP, United Kingdom
Reservations are limited to only a few dates a year. To be notified about them, you must subscribe to the Living Architecture foundation newsletter:
living-architecture.co.uk/the-houses/a-house-for-essex/book
info@living-architecture.co.uk
(44) 0-203 488 1584
€€€

Grotte de la Cocalière 47
30500 Courry, France
04 66 24 34 74 (The booking service is open only in July and August, every day from 9.30 am to 6 pm)
accueil@grotte-cocaliere.com
€€€

Château du Val d'Arguenon 49
Rue du Val, 22380 Saint-Cast-le-Guildo, France
chateau@chateauduval.com
chateauduval.com
€€

Villa Cheminée (Chimney Villa) 51
Le Grand Quartier, 44360 Cordemais, France
info@levoyageanantes.fr
levoyageanantes.fr/hebergements/villa-cheminee
€€

Buron of Niercombe 53
15800 Saint-Jacques-des-Blats, France
burons-gites-auvergne.com/F_niercombe.html
€€€

Cadoles de La Colline du Colombier 55
Le Colombier, 71340 Iguerande, France
troisgros.fr
la-colline-du-colombier@troisgros.com
€€€

Le Corbusier Hotel 57
280, boulevard Michelet, 13008 Marseille, France
hotellecorbusier.com
€€

Château Valmer 59
Château de Valmer,
81, boulevard de Gigaro,
83420 La Croix-Valmer, France
info@chateauvalmer.com
chateauvalmer.com/fr/chambres/cabanes/cabane-des-ecureuils
€€

CAB Foundation 61
5766, chemin des Trious,
06570 Saint-Paul-de-Vence,
France
fondationcab.com
spv@fondationcab.com
+33 4 921 124 49
€€€

Citerne-Lit 65
Lac de Guirande, 46270 Felzins,
France
greengo.voyage/hote/citerne-lit
€

Martin's Patershof Hotel 67
Karmelietenstraat 4,
2800 Malines,
Belgium
martinshotels.com
€€€

Hotel Inntel Zaandam 69
Provincialeweg 102,
1506 MD Zaandam,
Netherlands
infozaandam@inntelhotels.nl
inntelhotelsamsterdamzaandam.nl
€€

Marqués de Riscal 70
C/ Torrea 1, 01340 Elciego, Álava, Spain
marquesderiscal@marquesderiscal.com
marquesderiscal.com
€€€

Hotel Puerta América Madrid 75
Avenida de América, 41,
28002 Madrid, Spain
booking@puertamericahotel.com
hotelpuertamerica.com
€€

Circo Raluy Legacy 77
Plaça President Tarradellas, Badalona, Spain
info@circoraluy.com
circoraluy.com/hotel-con-encanto
€€

Palace Hotel Do Bussaco 79
Mata do Bussaco,
3050-261 Luso, Portugal
almeidahotels.pt/en/bussaco-palace-hotel
€€

Villa Crespi 83
Via Giuseppe Fava, 18,
28016 Orta San Giulio NO, Italy
info@villacrespi.it
villacrespi.it
€€

Atelier sul Mare 87
Via Cesare Battisti, 4,
98079 Castel di Tusa ME, Italy
info@ateliersulmare.it
ateliersulmare.com
€€

Principe di Savoia Hotel 89
Piazza della Repubblica 17, 20124 Milan, Italy
reservations.HPS@dorchestercollection.com
dorchestercollection.com/en/milan/hotel-principe-di-savoia
€€€

Villa Médicis 91
Viale della Trinità dei Monti,
00187 Rome, Italy
Reservations by e-mail only and no more than four months in advance: standard@villamedici.it (Specify that you wish to stay in a historic room; classic rooms, also located in the villa, are available at considerably lower rates)
villamedici.it/en/disvoer-and-visit-the-villa/rentals-guest-house
€€€

Hotel Ještěd 97
Horní Hanychov 153, 460 08 Liberec 8,
Czech Republic
recepce@jested.cz
jested.cz
€€

V8 Hotel 99
Charles-Lindbergh-Platz 1,
71034 Böblingen, Germany
info@v8hotel.de
v8hotel.de
€€

Rogner Bad Blumau 100
Bad Blumau 100, 8283 Bad Blumau,
Austria
urlaubsschneiderei@rogner.com
blumau.com
€€

Almdorf Seinerzeit 105
Vorderkoflach 36, 9564 Patergassen, Austria
welcome@almdorf.com
almdorf.com
€€€

Whitepod Eco-Luxury Hotel 107
Les Giettes, Des Cerniers, 1871 Monthey,
Switzerland
whitepod.com
€€€

Iglu-Dorf 109
Iglu-Dorf GmbH, Rotzbergstrasse 15,
6362 Stansstad, Switzerland
info@iglu-dorf.com
iglu-dorf.com
€€

Kolarbyn 111
Skärsjön, Fiskelevägen,
73030 Skinnskatteberg, Sweden
info@kolarbyn.se
kolarbyn.se/en/activity-romantic-adventure-in-charcoal-hut
€€

Treehotel 113
Edeforsväg 2 A, 960 24 Harads, Sweden
booking@treehotel.se
treehotel.se
€€€

Jumbo Stay 119
Jumbovägen 4,
SE-190 47 Stockholm Arlanda, Sweden
booking@jumbostay.com
jumbostay.com
€€

Icehotel 121
Marknadsvägen 63, 981 91 Jukkasjärvi, Sweden
info@icehotel.com
icehotel.com
€€€

Arctic Bath 123
Ramdalsvägen 10, 960 24 Harads, Sweden
booking@arcticbath.se
arcticbath.se
€€€

Manta Resort 129
Pemba Island, Zanzibar, Tanzania
direct@themantaresort.com
themantaresort.com
€€€

The Grand Daddy 133
38 Long Street, Cape Town, 8001,
South Africa
info@granddaddy.co.za
granddaddy.co.za
€€

Kaggakamma Hotel 135
Latitude : 32°44'49.68''S
Longitude : 19°33'46.94''E
South Africa
reservations@kaggakamma.co.za
kaggakamma.co.za
€€€

Kruger Shalati 139
Selati Station & Bridge, Skukuza Rest Camp,
Kruger National Park, PO box 360
Skukuza 1350, South Africa
reservations@krugershalati.com
krugershalati.com
€€€

Hippo Point Wildlife Sanctuary 143
PO Box 1852, Naivasha, Kenya
hippopointkenya.com
casilda@hippopointkenya.com
€€€

Loisaba Star Bed 145
Latitude : 0°37'54.8"N
Longitude : 36°50'45.5"E
Nanyuki, Kenya
reservations@elewana.com
elewanacollection.com/loisaba-star-beds
€€€

Giraffe Manor 149
Gogo Falls Road, Nairobi, Kenya
info@thesafaricollection.com
thesafaricollection.com/properties/giraffe-manor
€€€

Niassam Hills Lodge 155
Palmarin Ngallou, BP 03 Palmarin, Senegal
niassam.com
€€

Atlantis, The Palm 157
Crescent Rd, The Palm Jumeirah, Dubai,
United Arab Emirates
reservations@atlantisdubai.com
atlantis.com/dubai/rooms-and-suites/signature-suites/underwater-suite
€€€

Ulpotha Yoga & Ayurveda Retreat 161
7.907945, 80.365928 Embogama,
60718, Sri Lanka
info@ulpotha.com
ulpotha.com
€€€

Taprobane Island 163
Weligama, Sri Lanka
info@thesunhouse.com
taprobaneisland.com
€€€

The Muraka Suite – Conrad Maldives
Rangali Island Resort 165
Rangali islands 20077, Maldives
conradmaldives.com
€€€

Hang Nga Guesthouse 169
03 Đ. Huỳnh Thúc Kháng, Phường 4,
Thành phố Đà Lạt, Lâm Đồng 66115, Viêt Nam
reservation@crazyhouse.com.vn
crazyhouse.vn
€

Sheraton Huzhou Hot Spring Resort 171
No. 5858 Taihu Road,
Huzhou 313000, China
marriott.fr/hotels/travel/wuxsi-sheraton-huzhou-hot-spring-resort
€€€

Benesse Art House 175
Gotanji, Naoshima-cho,
Kagawa-gun 761-3110,
Kagawa Prefecture,
Japan
benesse-artsite.jp/en/stay
€€€

Treeful Treehouse Sustainable
Resort 177
2578 Genka, Nago-shi -Okinawa,
Japan
info@treeful.net
treeful.net
€€€

House of Light 181
2891 Ueno-Ko,
Tokamachi,
Niigata 948-0122,
Japan
hikari01@hikarinoyakata.com
hikarinoyakata.com
€€

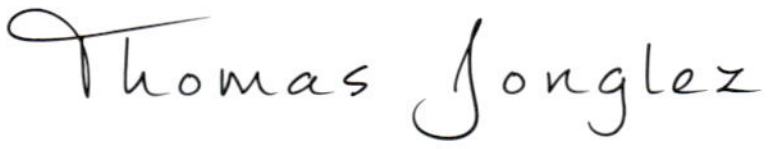

It was September 1995 and Thomas Jonglez was in Peshawar, the northern Pakistani city 20 kilometres from the tribal zone he was to visit a few days later. It occurred to him that he should record the hidden aspects of his native city, Paris, which he knew so well. During his seven-month trip back home from Beijing, the countries he crossed took in Tibet (entering clandestinely, hidden under blankets in an overnight bus), Iran and Kurdistan. He never took a plane but travelled by boat, train or bus, hitchhiking, cycling, on horseback or on foot, reaching Paris just in time to celebrate Christmas with the family.

On his return, he spent two fantastic years wandering the streets of the capital to gather material for his first 'secret guide', written with a friend. For the next seven years he worked in the steel industry until the passion for discovery overtook him. He launched Jonglez Publishing in 2003 and moved to Venice three years later.

In 2013, in search of new adventures, the family left Venice and spent six months travelling to Brazil, via North Korea, Micronesia, the Solomon Islands, Easter Island, Peru and Bolivia.

After seven years in Rio de Janeiro, he now lives in Berlin with his wife and three children.

Jonglez Publishing produces a range of titles in nine languages, released in 40 countries.

From the same publisher

Atlas

Atlas of geographical curiosities

Photobooks

Abandoned America
Abandoned Asylums
Abandoned Australia
Abandoned USSR
Abandoned Churches: Unclaimed places of worship
Abandoned cinemas of the world
Abandoned France
Abandoned Italy
Abandoned Japan
Abandoned Spain
After the Final Curtain – The Fall of the American Movie Theater
After the Final Curtain – America's Abandoned Theaters
Baikonur - Vestiges of the Soviet space programme
Chernobyl's Atomic Legacy
Forbidden Places – Exploring our Abandoned Heritage Vol. 1
Forbidden Places – Exploring our Abandoned Heritage Vol. 2
Forbidden Places – Exploring our Abandoned Heritage Vol. 3
Forgotten Heritage
Oblivion
Unusual wines
Venice deserted

Guides 'Soul of'

Soul of Amsterdam – A guide to the 30 best experiences
Soul of Athens – A guide to 30 exceptional experiences
Soul of Berlin – A guide to the 30 best experiences
Soul of Kyoto – A guide to 30 exceptional experiences
Soul of Lisbon – A guide to 30 exceptional experiences
Soul of Los Angeles – A guide to 30 exceptional experiences
Soul of Marrakesh – A guide to 30 exceptional experiences
Soul of New York – A guide to 30 exceptional experiencess
Soul of Rome – A guide to 30 exceptional experiencess
Soul of Tokyo – A guide to 30 exceptional experiences

Secret guides

Secret Amsterdam
Secret Bali – An unusual guide
Secret Bangkok
Secret Barcelona
Secret Belfast
Secret Berlin
Secret Brighton – An unusual guide
Secret Brooklyn
Secret Brussels
Secret Buenos Aires
Secret Campania
Secret Cape Town
Secret Copenhagen
Secret Dublin – An unusual guide
Secret Edinburgh – An unusual guide
Secret Florence
Secret French Riviera
Secret Geneva
Secret Glasgow
Secret Granada
Secret Helsinki
Secret Istanbul
Secret Johannesburg
Secret Lisbon
Secret Liverpool – An unusual guide
Secret London – An unusual guide
Secret London – Unusual bars & restaurants
Secret Madrid
Secret Mexico City
Secret Milan
Secret Montreal – An unusual guide
Secret Naples
Secret New Orleans
Secret New York – An unusual guide
Secret New York – Curious activities
Secret New York – Hidden bars & restaurants
Secret Paris
Secret Prague
Secret Provence
Secret Rio
Secret Rome
Secret Singapore
Secret Sussex – An unusual guide
Secret Tokyo
Secret Tuscany
Secret Venice
Secret Vienna
Secret Washington D.C.
Secret York – An unusual guide

Follow us on Facebook, Instagram and Twitter

Copyrights:
Free Spirit Spheres ©Mallory Owen – Quinta Real Zacatecas ©2013 Quinta Real Hotels – Canopy Tower ©David Tipling/Canopy Tower, ©Canopy Tower, Photo : RAdP – Costa Verde ©Hotel Costa Verde – Magic Mountain Hotel ©Lodge Montaña Mágica, Reserva Biológica Huilo Huilo – Skylodge Adventure Suites ©Skylodge Adventures – The Egyptian House, Gothic Temple, The Pineapple ©The Landmark Trust – Balancing Barn ©Jack Hobhouse – The Gormley Suite of the Beaumont Hotel ©The Beaumont – House for Essex ©Jack Hobhouse – Le Carré Rouge, ©André Morin/le carré rouge – The Château du Val d'Arguenon's Tree Houses ©Cabanes du Château du Val d'Arguenon – Villa Cheminée, Tatzu Nishi, Bouée/Cordemais, création pérenne Estuaire Nantes <> Saint-Nazaire 2009 ©Gino Maccarinelli – Buron of Niercombe © le buron de Niercombe – Cadoles de La Colline du Colombier ©les Cadoles de La Colline du Colombier – Le Corbusier Hotel ©Hôtel Le Corbusier – The Château Valmer Tree House ©Jacques Garance – The Jean Prouvé room in the CAB Foundation ©Antoine Lippens – The Citerne-Lit ©Kristof Guez – The Best of Home suite in Martin's Patershof Hotel ©Martin's Hotels – Hotel Inntel Zaandam ©Inntel Hotels – Marqués de Riscal ©Angélica Heras (p. 70) and ©David Mapletoft (p. 72) – Hotel Puerta America, Hotel Silken Puerta America (Madrid) ©Rafael Vargas – Palace Hotel do Bussaco ©Thomas Jonglez – Villa Crespi ©Villa Crespi and © Francesca Pagliai – Atelier sul Mare ©ART Hotel Atelier sul Mare, ©Jacques Garance – The Presidential Suite at the Principe di Savoia Hotel ©Hotel Principe di Savoia – Villa Médicis ©Assaf Shoshan for Villa Médicis and ©Daniele Molajoli/ Villa Medici – Hôtel Ještěd, ©Hotel Ještěd – V8 Hotel ©FrankHoppe/V8 HOTEL im Meilenwerk – Rogner Bad Blumau, Architektur ©Rogner – Almdorf Seinerzeit Tree House ©Almdorf Seinerzeit – Whitepod Eco-Luxury Hotel ©Sofia de Meyer/Whitepod – Iglu-Dorf ©Iglu-Dorf – Kolarbyn, ©Kolarbyn/Photo : Mikaela Larm – Treehotel ©Peter Lundstrom, WDO – Jumbo Stay ©Oscar Diös – Icehotel ©Jacques Garance – Arctic Bath ©Swedish Lapland DJI, ©Malin Saxcom, ©Bilder, ©Viggo Lundberg, ©Norrland, ©Pasquale Baseotto and ©AlexAndJames – Manta Resort Underwater Room ©Manta Resort – The Grand Daddy ©2013 Granddaddy.com – The Sky Suite of Kaggakamma Hotel ©Hotel Kagga Kamma – Kruger Shalati ©Kruger Shalati – Hippo Point Wildlife Sanctuary ©Hippo Point (Management Ltd.) – Loisaba Star Bed ©2013 Loisaba Wilderness, Kenya – Giraffe Manor ©The Safari Collection – Niassam Hills Lodge © Lodge de Niassam/François Goudier ©Nicolas van Beek – Atlantis, The Palm ©Atlantis, The Palm – Ulpotha Yoga & Ayurveda Retreat ©Ulpotha Yoga & Ayurveda Retreat – Taprobane Island © Taprobane Island – The Muraka Suite of the Conrad Maldives Rangali Island Resort ©Justin Nicholas – Hang Nga Guesthouse ©2013 Madam Dang Viet Nga/Photo: Hoa Nguyen – Sheraton Huzhou Hot Spring Resort ©McLennan/SheratonHuzhou – Benesse Art House ©Nicolas van Beek, ©Benesse House, Photograph: Fujitsuka Mitsumasa, ©Shinro Ohtake, Stern with Hole, Photograph: Koji Murakami, ©Yayoi Kusama, Pumpkin, Photograph: Shigeo Anzai, ©Cai Guo-Qiang, Cultural Melting Bath Project for Naoshima, Photograph: Fujitsuka Mitsumasa, ©Kan Yasuda, The Secret of the Sky, Photograph: Tadasu Yamamoto, ©Art House Project Hiroshi Sugimoto, Go'o Shrine, Photograph: Hiroshi SugimotoCapsule Hotels, ©Jacques Garance – Treeful Treehouse Sustainable Resort ©Treeful Treehouse Sustainable Resort – House of Light ©House of Light.

Layout: Emmanuelle Willard Toulemonde – Translation: Olivia Fuller – Copy-editing/proof-reading: Caroline Lawrence, Jana Gough, Kimberly Bess, Lee Dickinson – Publishing: Clémence Mathé

Registration of copyright: October 2023 – Edition: 03
ISBN: 978-2-36195-674-5
Printed in Slovakia by Polygraf